The Easy 5-Ingredient Ketogenic Vegetarian Cookbook

Quick and Delicious Plant-Based Recipes for Rapid Weight Loss

Susan Brown

D1377245

Table of contents

By reading this document, the reader agrees that under no circumstances are we responsible for any losses, direct or indirect, which are incurred as a result of the use of information contained within this document, including, but not limited to, errors, omissions, or inaccuracies.

CHAPTER 1: UNDERSTANDING THE KETOGENIC DIET

"Say no to excessive carbohydrates" this Meta description comes with every other Ketogenic Diet plan, as this dietary map helps us reduce the daily intake of carbohydrates. The ketogenic diet is more than we assume it to be, it does not only prohibit the use of carbohydrates but also suggests additional intake of fats and maintains a healthy balance in our diet. Reading a comprehensive keto diet plan may make us believe that it is not for everyone but with clear understanding and proper guidance at every step it can turn out to be simple and easy. In fact, it is just the matter of the routine.For beginners, an all-out carb cut down is not probably a good idea, try with some minor changes every day and within a month you can easily switch to a complete Ketogenic Diet. To gain maximum health benefits out of this diet, ensure proper hydration, intake of fluids along with normal body exercises. It aids our body to swiftly adjust according to the diet changes. The key is to keep 70% fats and about 5 % of carbohydrates in your diet. Besides the basic concept, there are many aspects about the Ketogenic diet which are important discuss. From its origin to contemporary studies ketosis and ketogenic diet amaze all due to the miraculous effects it has brought. Diseases which were not even cured through the use of modern day medications can now be treated and cured using a set of dietary plans.

The History of Ketogenic Diet

The rise of ketogenic diet dates back to 1920 to 1930s as a food therapy for epilepsy, a brain-related disease. Unlike other medicated treatments, the ketogenic worked due to its long-lasting impact. It emerged as a good alternative to fasting, which was earlier used to treat epilepsy. But the idea of keto therapy soon faced a failure due to lack of research and extensive use of medications.

However, in 1921, Rollin Woodyatt revived the idea of ketogenic diet and brought its benefits back in the spotlight when is spotted the three important compounds being produced in the bodies of those who either fast or eat low carb and high-fat diet. Soon Russel Wilder termed such a diet as "Ketogenic" due to its known effects of producing a high number of ketones in the body. From that point on, the concept of Ketosis prevailed. It was however got to the public attention as late as 1997 when Charlie Abraham's epilepsy was treated through the use of a complete Ketogenic Diet plan. The interest of the scientific community and ordinary individuals in the study of the ketogenic study came to the rise by 2007, the idea spread to up to 45 countries around the world. People actively sought to this diet plan, not only to treat specific diseases by also to reduce weight and avoid cardiovascular disease.

The Ketosis Process

The word ketosis comes from the word "ketone", it is described as the process during which fats are broken down in the body to produce energy and Ketones. A high level of ketosis means the greater number of ketones in the body. In the absence of carbohydrates, the fats are forced to break down and produce ketones which are highly beneficial for active metabolism. To make this all happen, a special meal plan is required known as "Ketogenic diet." It describes a sum whole of all the eatables which are low in carbs and high in fats. Thus, allowing the body to extract energy directly from fats and not from the glucose. The diet plan is prescribed to treat a number of diseases like diabetes, epilepsy, obesity and heart problems.

However, there are certain complexities related to this diet as and it should always be opted with the guidance of a professional nutritionist, at least at the beginning when it is essential to learn about the basics of ketosis and the right approach to switch to a balance ketogenic diet.

Important Facts about Ketosis:

To understand ketosis more deeply and to sum it all, let's go through some important facts about ketosis.

- Ketosis only occurs in complete absence of glucose.
- It is a process in which are stored fats are actively broken down into released energy and ketones as a by-product.
- Keeping a balanced approach while following a ketogenic plan is utmost important else it can also cause Ketosis which leads to ketoacidosis and it can be fatal.
- People with type 1 diabetes especially are more prone to develop ketoacidosis, therefore it is not suggested to type 1 patients. And every person recommended following the diet after consulting an expert.

Levels of Ketogenic Diet:

To help understand the effects of ketogenic diet and the steady change towards adopting it new food style, experts have divided the entire cycle into three major phases. These include the induction phase, adjustment phase and fitness phase. These phases chalk out a complete roadmap to a full fledge keto routine.

1. Induction Phase:

Entering into the world of ketogenic diet require more of the mental strength than physical. It is important to prepare your mind for it and then act on it. Thus, the first phase is all about preparing yourself for this special diet. An easy way to do that is by removing all the possible high carb food items from your groceries and opting for more clean carbs. Do your research and plan things out for yourself. Be more steady and gradual to have a more lasting impact. Start limiting the number of carbs and keep track of the fats intake. Habit and discipline are most important while surviving through this phase. Loss of will means loss of efforts, so start sticking to the routine.

2. Adjustment Phase:

Now that induction phase has passed, the adjustment phase allows a person to add more variety to the diet using a variety of keto friendly fruits and vegetables. It is safe to add more fats to the diet through cream, cheeses or vegetable oils. In this phase the body goes through slight changes in terms of energy levels and health, thus adjustment in the diet is important to keep up with the pace of those changes.

3: Fitness Phase:

The last phase of this process is the fitness phase. By this time, the routine for keto diet must be well developed. However, the body still needs a kick start to burn more fans than glucose. A little exercise is recommended at this stage to help achieve the aim. Such exercise may range from light intensity aerobics to high-intensity exercises. Physical exercises together with a planned ketogenic diet are the road to healthy and active life.

Benefits of Ketogenic Diet

Being smart about our diet and health is the need of the hour. In today's ever busy lifestyle quality of food and diet is greatly compromised. Thus, having a good diet plan is crucial to maintain our health and prevent fatal diseases. There are many known benefits of ketogenic diet, most of us are unaware of. From better mental condition to improved health, the diet plan has proven to be miraculous in effect.

- Body Weight

Weight loss is one of the major reason many people opt for a ketogenic diet. And studies have proved that it does allow greater weight reduction in a much easier way. It not only helps in losing weight but also helps to tone our muscles and body shape.

- Cholesterol and Sugar Control

  Sugar control is important for patients with type 2 diabetes and keto is complete abstain you from sugars. Instead, special sweeteners are used to maintain the flavour. The diet is also effective in controlling the cholesterol level in the body.

- Better Mental State

  Ketones are knowns as the fuel for mind and ketosis ensure the production of ketones in a large amount in the body. Lesser intake of carbohydrates means the increased concentration of ketones.

- The cure for Seizures

  As Ketogenic diet was originally emerged to treat epileptic patients so it is known to control seizures or help to reduce them to some extent. Especially in children, it is effective alongside the medications.

- Blood Pressure

  As ketogenic diet helps to maintain high levels of triglyceride in the body it is also effective in controlling blood pressure and cholesterol levels. This, in turn, saves us from many fatal diseases, like cardiovascular diseases

- Help with Skin Problems

For people having skin problems, especially acne, this diet it one good solution. In the absence of complex carbohydrates, there is the minimal production of toxins in the blood, thus keep our skin healthy and acne free.

CHAPTER 2: VEGETARIAN DIET BASIC

What is the Vegetarian Diet?

You can define a vegetarian but defining a pure vegetarian diet is quite complex. The basic distinction is marked between meat and non-meat food. Any type of meat either red or white is strictly off the list but intake of eggs and dairy products doesn't fall into that category as many vegetarians prefer to take them in one form or other. Whereas some strict adherents of the vegetarian diet avoid all forms of animal produce even honey. So, in simple terms, a vegetarian diet largely consists of all the vegetables, fruits, pulses and grains.

Omitting meat altogether from the diet doesn't have any negative effects on our body. As pulses and beans are also good sources of protein. Moreover, a meatless diet means more fibres and fewer toxins. Further, it enables us to increase the intake of fruits and vegetables in the diet, which are more organic, fresh and natural. Such diet also boosts the metabolism and provide vital minerals and vitamins.

People who strictly follow a vegetarian diet are at lower risk of cardiovascular diseases, diabetes, obesity, cancer and experience longer active and healthy life. Animal fats are hard to digest due to their high saturation, they are more easily accumulated in the body within the vessels and other parts.

Advantages of the Vegetarian Diet

Among the many known benefits of a vegetarian diet, there are some more:

1. Reduces Risk of Cardiovascular Disease

According to many medical types of research, vegetarian shows lower risks of cardiovascular diseases than non-vegetarians and the reason is quite obvious, a diet rich in fruits and vegetable is also full of antioxidants. These agents are responsible for stopping atherosclerosis. Moreover, low levels of saturated fats do not cause any obstruction in the blood flow.

2. Low Cholesterol

Eating animal fat is like deliberately increasing the blood cholesterol levels, which is not good when it comes to health. After years of research in the field, the Korean Researchers proved that the vegetarians have low levels of cholesterols in their bodies compared to omnivores or the people who eat meat.

3. Less Risk of Stroke and Obesity

You are what you eat, it means our eating choices and habits directly impact the mind and the body. If you are not being smart about it, you will end up suffering from obesity or other diseases related to. Taking animal fats on regular bases is a known cause of obesity. There break down is comparatively slow, thus they accumulate in the body, sometimes even inside the veins causing a fatal stroke. Being vegetarian saves us from all that trouble.

4. Less Chance of Developing Kidney Stones

Breakdown of animal protein releases Uric acid in a large amount. Thus, experts are of the view that animal proteins can also be responsible for kidney stones. A diet free of animal protein can also prevent kidney stones.

5. Improved Mood

Interestingly, our diet also affects our mood. According to the research food from animal sources contain Arachidonic acid, which is related to the mood swings or disturbances. Thus, by avoiding meat, you can avoid arachidonic acid which enlightens the mood.

6. Improve Symptoms of Psoriasis

Psoriasis, a skin condition characterized by skin redness and irritation can also be treated using a vegetarian diet. Even a gradual shift from non-veg to a purely vegetarian diet has shown marked improvement in its patients.

7. Reduced Incidence of Diabetes

People suffering from type 2 diabetes are recommended to opt this diet plan to control their blood sugar levels. Research has also shown that people following a ketogenic diet, showed a marked balance in their blood sugar level without the use of any medication.

8. Nutritional Requirements

If someone is still confused about the nutritional value of the vegetarian diet then don't be, as it has also the essential nutrients required by human body. From proteins to fibers, carbs, fats, minerals and vitamin.

CHAPTER3: THE KETOGENIC VEGETARIAN DIET

A ketogenic vegetarian diet means looking for low carb alternative while abstaining from meat or animal produce. It may sound not so simple but with minor changes and clear idea of Keto Dos and Don'ts everyone can make it happen. With a deep understanding of vegetarian and keto diet substitute, you can enjoy every other recipe without the fear of all those carbohydrates.

Food to Eat:

To make things simple and easier, let's break it down a little and try to understand the Keto vegetarian diet plan as a chart explaining what to have and what not to have. Down below is a brief list of all the items which can be used on a Ketogenic vegetarian diet.

- Keto Friendly Vegetables:

  Keep this in mind that not all vegetables are low on carbs. There are some which are full of starch and they need to be avoided. A simple technique to access the suitability of the vegetables for a keto diet is to check if they are 'grown above the ground' or 'below it'. All vegetables which are grown underground are a no go for Keto whereas vegetables which are grown above are best for keto and these mainly include cauliflower, broccoli, zucchini, etc.

- Vegetarian "meats":

  To substitute meat in most of the recipes these are most opted Vegan meats tempeh, tofu and seifan. These can be cooked easily and tastes equally delicious.

- Green Vegetables:

  Among the vegetables, all the leafy green vegetables can be added to this diet which includes spinach, kale, parsley, cilantro etc.

- Seeds and Dry Nuts:

Nuts and seeds like sunflower seeds, pistachios, pumpkin seeds, almonds etc. can all be used on a ketogenic diet.

- Dairy Products:

  Not every dairy product is allow on a keto diet. For example, milk is a no go for keto whereas hard cheeses, high fat cream, butter, eggs, etc. can all be used.

- Keto Friendly Fruits:

  Not all berries are Keto friendly, only choose blackberries or raspberries, and other low carb berries. Similarly, not all fruits can be taken on a keto diet, avocado, coconut etc. are keto friendly whereas orange, apples and pineapple etc. are high in carbohydrates.

- Vegetable Fats:

  Following oils and fats can be used on a ketogenic diet: olive oil, coconut oil, palm oil, etc.

- Special Sweeteners:

  As sugar is strictly forbidden for a ketogenic diet, may it be brown or white there are a certain substitute which can be used like stevia, erythritol, monk fruit, and another low-carb sweetener

Table: Food to Eat

Vegetables	Fruits	Nuts	Healthy Oils	Dairy
Artichoke hearts	Avocados	Almonds	Almond oil	Coconut milk
Arugula	Blueberries*	Brazil nuts	Avocado oil	Almond milk
Asparagus	Coconuts	Hazelnuts/filberts	Cacao butter	Coconut cream
Bell peppers	Cranberries	Macadamia nuts	Coconut oil	Vegan butter

Beets	Lemons	Pecans	Flaxseed oil	Cheeses
Bok choy	Limes	Peanuts	Hazelnut oil	Silken Tofu
Broccoli	Olives	Pine nuts	Macadamia nut oil	
Brussels sprouts	Raspberries	Walnuts	MCT oil	
Cabbage	Strawberries	Chia	Olive oil	
Carrots	Tomatoes	Hemp	Healthy Oils	
Cauliflower	Watermelon	Pumpkin	Almond oil	
Celery				

Food Not to Eat:

Avoiding carbohydrate is the main aim of following a ketogenic diet. While most vegetarians may take following food items on a regular basis but they are considered as Keto Friendly. In fact any amount these items, drastically increased the carbohydrate value of your meal. So, it is best to avoid their use completely.

1. Grains:

All types of grains are high in carbohydrates, whether its rice or corn or wheat. And product extracting out them is equally high in carbs, like cornflour, wheat flour or rice flour. So, while you need to avoid these grains for keto, their flours should also be avoided. Almond and coconut flours are a good substitute for that.

2. Legumes:

Legumes are also the underground parts of the plants; thus, they are highly rich in carbohydrates. Make no mistake of using them in your diet. These include all sorts of beans, from Lima to chickpeas, Garbanzo, black, white, red beans etc. cross all of them off your grocery list if you are about to go keto. All types of lentils are also not allowed on a keto diet.

3. Sugar:

Besides white and brown sugar there are other forms of it which are also not keto friendly, this list includes honey, agave, maple syrup etc. Also, avoid chocolates which are high in sugar. Use special sweeteners and sugar-free chocolates only.

4. Fruits:

Certain fruits need to be avoided while on a keto diet. Apples, bananas, oranges, pineapple etc. all fall into that category. Do not use them in any form. Avoid using their flesh, juice and mash to keep your meal carb free.

5. Tubers:

Tubers are basically the underground vegetables and some of them are rich in carbs including potatoes, yams, sweet potatoes, beets etc.

6. Dairy:

As stated above, not all dairy product can be freely used on a ketogenic diet. Animal milk should be strictly avoided.

Table: Food Not to Eat

Grains	Legumes	Sugars	Fruits	Tubers	Dairy
Rice	Lentils	White	Apples	Yams	Animal Milk
Wheat	Chickpeas	brown	Banana	Potatoes	
Corn	Black beans	Maple syrup	Pineapples	Beets	
Barley	Garbanzo beans	agave	Oranges		
Millet	Lima Beans	honey	Pears		
Oats	Kidney beans	Confectioner's sugar	Pomegranate		
Quinoa	White beans	Granulated sugar	Watermelon		

CHAPTER 4: TIPS & FAQS

In a nutshell, following a keto vegetarian diet is more about the understanding of the plan and self. It is always important to first analyse the individual bodily requirements and health conditions and then switch to a diet plan. Here are some important tips for those who are new to the ketogenic diet and having trouble incorporating a complete ketogenic vegetarian diet into their routine.

Important Tips

1. Get Adapted:

The early period of the ketogenic diet is always crucial. Getting adapted to the routine does sound difficult but the faster you get through with it the easier it gets. Initially, when the sugars are completely removed from the diet it may even cause a Keto flu, which forces a person to switch back to the old ways. The key is to keep pushing it forward, do not stop and turn around, care for your health and set the mind to achieve the target.

2. Complete Routine:

Ketogenic diet plan doesn't only include a three times meal a day plan for everyone. This plan also requires you to take more minerals like sodium and magnesium along with other electrolytes. Thus, drink more water and keep the body hydrated. Moreover, exercise daily to boost the fat burning process in your body.

3. Food Quality:

Cutting on the carbs doesn't mean to comprise on the quality of the food. It only restricts the amount, so make sure that it is high quality. Keep check of the calories and do not skip any meal during the day.

4. No Keto Strips:

Many people prescribe the use of keto strips to detect the number of ketones in the blood or urine and keep track of them. But it is not important if you are strictly following the routine and taking low levels of carbohydrates. For those who have special health conditions or problems can, however, use these strips.

5. No Cheating:

There comes a time during the early stages of ketogenic cycle whereas person feels discouraged and lose control of the diet routine. No cheating is the key to a better health, even a single meal with high crabs can make your entire struggle go in vain.

6. Clearance from Doctor:

A proper medical check-up and consultation with a doctor are important before starting ketogenic diet. Only a doctor or an expert can determine the bodily requirements and deficiencies. As the ketosis may vary from individual and depends on the rate of metabolism, only a doctor can properly guide us in the right direction.

Frequently Asked Question

What is the difference between a low-carbohydrate diet and a ketogenic diet?

Low carbohydrate diet is a general term used to describe any diet containing 130 to 150 grams on the total. However ketogenic diets are the subset of this general diet plan. It further restricts the amount of carbohydrate to minimum levels and at the same time requires an increased intake of fat. Thus, a ketogenic diet plan is more specific than the low carbohydrate plan.

Do I need to count calories? Do calories matter?

Keeping track of caloric intake is important as it directly relates to weight gain. Whether on a low carb diet or on a high one, it is necessary to keep check of the calories.

How do I track my macros / my carb intake?

Whenever you follow a recipe, look for its contents and the nutritional value available with the recipe. If it is not available, look for online nutrition calculators which enables you to calculate the nutritional value within few minutes.

How long does it take to get to ketosis?

If you are a person of discipline and routine then it usually takes 2 to 3 days to start a keto routine. However, it is a gradual process and goes through different stages. Exercise helps boosts the speed of the process. For people with sedentary lifestyles, it can also take weeks.

Can I eat dairy?

This is perhaps the most frequently asked question by the people who are new to a keto diet. Not all dairy products are keto friendly as raw dairy products are high in carbs. But those fermented or processed loses their carbohydrates and are good to use, these include butter, cheese and yoghurt.

Can I eat fruit?

Yes, fruits like avocados, coconut and moderate amounts of low-carb fruits such as berries. Tomato which is a fruit can also be eaten in a balanced amount. However, fruits which are high in sugar should be avoided.

Which sweeteners can I use?

Using sweeteners is a tricky part of the ketogenic diet. While there many available in the market there are few which are mostly used like stevia, erythritol, swerve etc. These sweeteners are a good substitute for any sugar when used in the right proportion. As the sweetness of these sweeteners varies, always compare the proportions and then add to the recipe.

Are fermented foods allowed?

Yes, raw fermented foods like kimchi, kombucha, sauerkraut, kefir (dairy or coconut) or raw full-fat plain yoghurt are full of probiotics, vitamins and enzymes. They help in better digestion and strength the immunity system of the body. Their regular intake is vital for active metabolism.

Can I eat peanuts?

Not all legumes are not keto friendly, peanuts are one of them. There is a great misconception that peanuts can be taken on a keto diet, but it is clearly not true as they are low on carbs and high in fats. When taken in small amounts, they do not disrupt the balance of the ketogenic diet.

Is ketosis dangerous?

There is no proven evidence which could suggest that ketosis is dangerous. Many people confuse ketosis with the ketoacidosis, the latter is a health problem which only occurs in patients with diabetes type 1. During ketoacidosis, the ketones level in the blood exceeds up to a critical value. Ketosis, on the other hand, is completely normal and doesn't pose any danger to a person's health.

Aren't high-fat diets unhealthy? Isn't eating so much fat going to make me fat?

Most of us believe that high fats are unhealthy but it is nothing but a myth. Fats can only be unhealthy if taken with the high amount of carbohydrates. However, when taken with low carbs or no carbs, these fats become a direct and active source of energy for the body. They easily break down and releases essential compounds including ketones.

CHAPTER 5: KETOGENIC BREAKFAST
Tofu Mushrooms

Prep Time: 5 minutes

Cooking Time: 10 minutes

Servings: 3

Ingredients:

- 1 block tofu, pressed and diced into 1-inch pieces
- 1 cup fresh mushrooms, chopped finely
- 4 tablespoons butter
- 4 tablespoons Parmesan cheese, shredded
- Salt and freshly ground black pepper, to taste

Method:

1. Season tofu cubes with salt and black pepper in a bowl.
2. Heat butter in a pan and add the tofu to sauté for 5 minutes.
3. Stir in mushrooms and Parmesan cheese. Continue cooking for 5 minutes.
4. Stir well and serve warm.

Nutritional Information per Serving:

- Calories 211
- Total Fat 18.5 g
- Saturated Fat 11.5 g
- Cholesterol 51 mg
- Total Carbs 2 g
- Sugar 0.5 g
- Fibre 0.4 g
- Sodium 346 mg
- Potassium 93 mg
- *Protein 11.5 g*

Onion Tofu

Prep Time: 8 minutes

Cooking Time: 5 minutes

Servings: 3

Ingredients:

- 2 blocks tofu, pressed and cubed into 1 inch pieces
- 2 medium onions, sliced
- 2 tablespoons butter
- 1 cup cheddar cheese, grated
- Salt and freshly ground black pepper, to taste

Method:

1. Season the tofu with salt and black pepper in a bowl.
2. Melt butter in a pan and add onions to sauté for 3 minutes.
3. Stir in seasoned tofu and cook for 2 minutes.
4. Add cheddar cheese and cover the pan to cook for 5 minutes on low heat.
5. Serve warm.

Nutritional Information per Serving:

- Calories 184
- Total Fat 12.7 g
- Saturated Fat 7.3 g
- Cholesterol 35 mg
- Total Carbs 6.3 g
- Sugar 2.7 g
- Fibre 1.6 g
- Sodium 222 mg
- Potassium 174 mg
- Protein 12.2 g

Spinach Rich Ballet

Prep Time: 5 minutes

Cooking Time: 30 minutes

Servings: 4

Ingredients:

- 1½ pounds fresh baby spinach
- 8 teaspoons coconut cream
- 14-ounces cauliflower, sliced
- 2 tablespoons unsalted butter, melted
- Salt and freshly ground black pepper, to taste

Method:

1. Preheat your oven to 360 degrees F.
2. Melt butter in a skillet and add spinach to sauté for 3 minutes.
3. Drain excess liquid and transfer the spinach to 4 greased ramekins.
4. Add cauliflower, cream, salt and pepper to the ramekins.
5. Bake for 25 minutes then serve warm.

Nutritional Information per Serving:

- Calories 188
- Total Fat 12.5 g
- Saturated Fat 4.4 g
- Cholesterol 53 mg
- Total Carbs 4.9 g
- Sugar 0.3 g
- Fibre 2 g
- Sodium 1098 mg
- Potassium 484 mg
- *Protein 14.6 g*

Pepperoni Egg Omelet

Prep Time: 5 minutes

Cooking Time: 20 minutes

Servings: 4

Ingredients:

- 15 pepperoni slices
- 6 eggs
- 2 tablespoons butter
- 4 tablespoons coconut cream
- Salt and freshly ground black pepper, to taste

Method:

1. Whisk eggs with all the remaining ingredients in a bowl.
2. Heat butter in a skillet.
3. Pour the ¼ of the egg mixture into the skillet. Cook for 2 minutes per side.
4. Repeat to use the entire batter.
5. Serve warm.

Nutritional Information per Serving:

- Calories 141
- Total Fat 11.3 g
- Saturated Fat 3.8 g
- Cholesterol 181 mg
- Total Carbs 0.6 g
- Sugar 0.5 g
- Fiber 0 g
- Sodium 334 mg
- Potassium 103 mg
- Protein 8.9 g

Nut Porridge

Prep Time: 10 minutes

Cooking Time: 15 minutes

Servings: 4

Ingredients:

- 1 cup cashew nuts, raw and unsalted
- 1 cup pecan, halved
- 2 tablespoons stevia
- 4 teaspoons coconut oil, melted
- 2 cups water

Method:

1. Chop all the pecans and cashews in the food processor until it forms a smooth powder.
2. Add water, oil and stevia to the nuts powder.
3. Transfer the mixture to a saucepan. Stir cook for 5 minutes on high heat.
4. Reduce the heat to low and let it simmer for 10 minutes.
5. Serve warm and enjoy.

Nutritional Information per Serving:

- Calories 260
- Total Fat 22.9 g
- Saturated Fat 7.3 g
- Cholesterol 0 mg
- Total Carbs 12.7 g
- Sugar 1.8 g
- Fiber 1.4 g
- Sodium 9 mg
- Potassium 209 mg

- *Protein 5.6 g*

Parsley Soufflé

Prep Time: 5 minutes

Cooking Time: 6 minutes

Servings: 1

Ingredients:

- 2 eggs
- 1 fresh red chilli pepper, chopped
- 2 tablespoons coconut cream
- 1 tablespoon fresh parsley, chopped
- Salt, to taste

Method:

1. Preheat your oven to 390 degrees F and butter 2 soufflé dishes.
2. Blend all the ingredients together in a blender.
3. Divide the batter into soufflé dishes.
4. Bake for 6 minutes and serve.

Nutritional Information per Serving:

- Calories 108
- Total Fat 9 g
- Saturated Fat 4.3 g
- Cholesterol 180 mg
- Total Carbs 1.1 g
- Sugar 0.5 g
- Fiber 0.1 g
- Sodium 146 mg
- Potassium 89 mg
- *Protein 6 g*

Bok Choy Samba

Prep Time: 5 minutes

Cooking Time: 15 minutes

Servings: 3

Ingredients:

- 1 onion sliced
- 4 bok choy, sliced
- 4 tablespoons coconut cream
- Salt and freshly ground black pepper, to taste
- ½ cup Parmesan cheese, grated

Method:

1. Mix bok choy with salt and black pepper.
2. Heat oil in a pan and add onion slice to sauté for 5 minutes.
3. Add cream and seasoned bok choy. Cook for 6 minutes.
4. Stir in Parmesan cheese and cover the lid.
5. Reduce the heat to low and cook for 3 minutes.
6. Serve warm.

Nutritional Information per Serving:

- Calories 112
- Total Fat 4.9 g
- Saturated Fat 1.9 g
- Cholesterol 10 mg
- Total Carbs 1.9 g
- Sugar 0.8 g
- Fibre 0.4 g
- Sodium 355 mg
- Potassium 101 mg

- *Protein 3 g*

Eggs with Watercress

Prep Time: 10 minutes

Cooking Time: 5 minutes

Servings: 6

Ingredients:

- 6 organic eggs, boiled, peeled and cut in half lengthwise
- 1 medium ripe avocado, peeled, pitted and chopped
- 1/3 cup fresh watercress, trimmed
- ½ tablespoon fresh lemon juice
- Salt, to taste

Method:

1. Set a trivet at the bottom of the Instant Pot and pour 1 cup water into
2. Arrange the watercress on the trivet and seal the lid.
3. Select "Manual" function with high pressure for 3 minutes.
4. When the timer goes off, quickly release the pressure.
5. Drain the watercress
6. Mix watercress with egg yolks, lemon juice, avocado and salt in a bowl. Use a fork to mash the mixture.
7. Spoon the mixture into the remaining egg whites.
8. Serve and enjoy.

Nutritional Information per Serving:

- Calories 132
- Total Fat 10.9 g
- Saturated Fat 2.7 g
- Cholesterol 164 mg
- Total Carbs 3.3 g

- Sugar 0.5 g
- Fibre 2.3 g
- Sodium 65 mg
- Potassium 226 mg
- *Protein 6.3 g*

CHAPTER 6: KETOGENIC LUNCH
Creamy Leeks

Prep Time: 10 minutes

Cooking Time: 25 minutes

Servings: 6

Ingredients:

- 1½ lbs. leeks, trimmed and chopped into 4-inch pieces
- 2 oz. butter
- 1 cup coconut cream
- 3½ oz. cheddar cheese
- salt and pepper to taste

Method:

1. Preheat the oven to 400°F (200°C).
2. Heat butter in a skillet over medium heat.
3. Add leeks to sauté for 5 minutes.
4. Spread the leeks to in a greased baking dish.
5. Boil cream in a saucepan then reduces the heat to low.
6. Stir in cheese, salt and pepper.
7. Pour this sauce over the leeks.
8. Bake for about 15 to 20 minutes.
9. Serve warm.

Nutritional Information per Serving:

- Calories 204
- Total Fat 15.7 g
- Saturated Fat 9.7 g
- Cholesterol 49 mg

- Total Carbs 12.6 g
- Sugar 3.4 g
- Fibre 1.5 g
- Sodium 141 mg
- Potassium 178 mg
- *Protein 6.3 g*

Parmesan Croutons

Prep Time: 10 minutes

Cooking Time: 40 minutes

Servings: 8

Ingredients:

- 1 ½ cups almond flour
- 2 teaspoons baking powder
- 1 teaspoon sea salt
- 1¼ cups boiling water
- 3 egg whites
- Parmesan cheese (garnish)

Method:

1. Preheat the oven to 350°F (175°C).
2. Mix almond flour with salt and baking powder in a bowl.
3. Whisk egg whites and add to the dry mixture.
4. Mix well until it forms a smooth dough.
5. Prepare 8 flat pieces of dough using moist hands.
6. Arrange the flattened dough on a baking sheet with some distance apart.
7. Bake them for about 40 minutes.
8. Sprinkle parmesan cheese on top and bake for 5 minutes.
9. Serve and enjoy.

Nutritional Information per Serving:

- Calories 156
- Total Fat 11.7 g
- Saturated Fat 1.8 g
- Cholesterol 5 mg

- Total Carbs 5.4 g
- Sugar 0.1 g
- Fibre 2.3 g
- Sodium 323 mg
- Potassium 147 mg
- *Protein 8.1 g*

Quesadillas

Prep Time: 10 minutes

Cooking Time: minutes

Servings: 4

Ingredients:

- 4 low carb tortillas, cut into small pieces
- 5 oz. grated Mexican cheese
- 1 oz. leafy greens
- 1 tablespoon olive oil, for frying
- Salt and pepper to taste

Method:

1. Heat oil in a pan over medium heat.
2. Spread half of the tortilla pieces in the pan and top them with half of the cheese and leafy greens.
3. Drizzle remaining cheese on top and add another layer of tortillas.
4. Cook for 1 minutes then flip to cook for another minute.
5. Slice it into eatable chunks.
6. Serve.

Nutritional Information per Serving:

- Calories 238
- Total Fat 16.9 g
- Saturated Fat 16.9 g
- Cholesterol 32 mg
- Total Carbs 13.5 g
- Sugar 0.1 g
- Fibre 7.2 g
- Sodium 469 mg

- Potassium 0 mg
- *Protein 10.8 g*

Cheesy Cauliflower

Prep Time: 10 minutes

Cooking Time: 25 minutes

Servings: 3

Ingredients:

- 1 cauliflower head
- ¼ cup butter, cut into small pieces
- 1 teaspoon mayonnaise
- 1 tablespoon prepared mustard
- ½ cup Parmesan cheese, grated

Method:

1. Preheat your oven to 390 degrees F.
2. Combine mayonnaise and mustard in a bowl.
3. Add cauliflower to the mayonnaise mixture. Mix well.
4. Spread the cauliflower in a baking dish and top it with butter.
5. Sprinkle with cheese on top and bake for about 25 minutes.
6. Serve warm.

Nutritional Information per Serving:

- Calories 228
- Total Fat 20.2 g
- Saturated Fat 12.5 g
- Cholesterol 54 mg
- Total Carbs 6 g
- Sugar 2.3 g
- Fibre 2.4 g
- Sodium 250 mg
- Potassium 280 mg

Parmesan Roasted Bamboo Sprouts

Prep Time: 10 minutes

Cooking Time: 15 minutes

Servings: 3

Ingredients:

- pound bamboo sprouts
- 2 tablespoons butter
- 1 cup Parmesan cheese, grated
- ¼ teaspoon paprika
- Salt and freshly ground black pepper, to taste

Method:

1. Preheat your oven to 350 degrees F and grease a baking dish then set it aside
2. Mix butter, paprika, salt and black pepper in a bowl.
3. Add green beans to the butter marinade and mix well. Marinate for 1 hour.
4. Transfer the mixture to the baking dish and bake for 15 minutes.
5. Serve.

Nutritional Information per Serving:

- Calories 193
- Total Fat 15.8 g
- Saturated Fat 10.3 g
- Cholesterol 47 mg
- Total Carbs 2.1 g
- Sugar 0.4 g
- Fibre 0.4 g
- Sodium 421 mg
- Potassium 6 mg
- Protein 12.6 g

Brussels Sprout with Lemon

Prep Time: 10 minutes

Cooking Time: 0 minute

Servings: 4

Ingredients:

- 1 lb. Brussels sprouts, trimmed and shredded
- 8 tablespoons olive oil
- 1 lemon, juice and zest
- salt and pepper
- 2/5 - ¾ cup spicy almond & seed mix or your own choice of nuts and seeds

Method:

1. Mix lemon juice with salt, pepper and olive in a bowl.
2. Stir in shredded Brussels sprouts. Mix well and let it sit for 10 minutes.
3. Add nuts mixture to the sprouts.
4. Serve.

Nutritional Information per Serving:

- Calories 382
- Total Fat 36.5 g
- Saturated Fat 5.5 g
- Cholesterol 0 mg
- Total Carbs 14.6 g
- Sugar 3.4 g
- Fibre 5.5 g
- Sodium 73 mg
- Potassium 539 mg
- *Protein 6.3 g*

Cauliflower Hash Browns

Prep Time: 10 minutes

Cooking Time: 30 minutes

Servings: 4

Ingredients:

- 1 lb. cauliflower, trimmed and grated
- 3 eggs
- ½ yellow onion, grated
- Salt and black pepper to taste
- 4 oz. butter, for frying

Method:

1. Whisk eggs in a bowl and add onion, cauliflower, salt and pepper.
2. Heat butter in the skillet over medium heat.
3. Add the batter spoon by spoon to the butter and spread the batter into 3 to 4-inch diameter circle
4. Cook for 3 to 5 minutes per side.
5. Use the entire batter to repeat the process.
6. Serve warm.

Nutritional Information per Serving:

- Calories 284
- Total Fat 26.4 g
- Saturated Fat 15.6 g
- Cholesterol 184 mg
- Total Carbs 7.6 g
- Sugar 3.6 g
- Fibre 3.1 g
- Sodium 244 mg

- Potassium 415 mg
- *Protein 6.8 g*

Cauliflower Parmesan

Prep Time: 10 minutes

Cooking Time: 25 minutes

Servings: 4

Ingredients:

- 1½ lbs. cauliflower, trimmed and sliced
- 2 tablespoons olive oil
- salt to taste
- Black pepper, to taste
- 4 oz. grated parmesan cheese

Method:

1. Preheat the oven to 400°F (200°C).
2. Arrange the cauliflower slices on a baking sheet lined with parchment paper.
3. Drizzle salt, pepper, olive oil and parmesan cheese on top.
4. Bake for about 20 to 25 minutes.
5. Serve warm.

Nutritional Information per Serving:

- Calories 278
- Total Fat 20.7 g
- Saturated Fat 5.7 g
- Cholesterol 44 mg
- Total Carbs 7.2 g
- Sugar 3.1 g
- Fibre 1.5 g
- Sodium 232 mg
- Potassium 416 mg
- *Protein 6.4 g*

Cauliflower Mash

Prep Time: 10 minutes

Cooking Time: 5 minutes

Servings: 4

Ingredients:

- 1 lb. cauliflower, cut into florets
- 3 oz. whipped heavy cream
- 4 oz. butter
- ½ lemon, juice and zest
- olive oil (optional)

Method:

1. Boil water along with salt in a saucepan.
2. Add cauliflower to the water and cook until soft.
3. Drain and transfer the cauliflower to a blender.
4. Add all the remaining ingredients and blend until smooth.
5. Serve.

Nutritional Information per Serving:

- Calories 337
- Total Fat 34.5 g
- Saturated Fat 20 g
- Cholesterol 90 mg
- Total Carbs 7.3 g
- Sugar2.9 g
- Fibre 3 g
- Sodium 206 mg
- Potassium 378 mg
- *Protein 3 g*

Halloumi Burger

Prep Time: 10 minutes

Cooking Time: 0 minute

Servings: 4

Ingredients:

- 15 oz. halloumi cheese
- butter or coconut oil
- 6 2/3 tablespoons sour cream
- 6 2/3 tablespoons mayonnaise
- Sliced vegetables, of your choice

Method:

1. Mix sour cream with mayonnaise in a bowl and cover the bowl. Refrigerate until further use.
2. Melt butter in a skillet and add halloumi cheese to cook until soft and light brown.
3. Place the cheese on the platter and top it with mayo mixture and vegetables.
4. Serve.

Nutritional Information per Serving:

- Calories 534
- Total Fat 45.1 g
- Saturated Fat 26.4 g
- Cholesterol 102 mg
- Total Carbs 9.4 g
- Sugar 4.3 g
- Fibre 0 g
- Sodium 740 mg
- Potassium 199 mg
- Protein 23.8 g

Creamy Green Cabbage

Prep Time: 10 minutes

Cooking Time: 10 minutes

Servings: 4

Ingredients:

- 2 oz. butter
- 1½ lbs. green cabbage, shredded
- 1¼ cups coconut cream
- salt and pepper
- 8 tablespoons fresh parsley, finely chopped

Method:

1. Heat butter in a skillet and add cabbage to sauté until golden brown.
2. Stir in cream and bring it to a simmer.
3. Add salt and pepper for seasoning.
4. Garnish with parsley.
5. Serve warm.

Nutritional Information per Serving:

- Calories 432
- Total Fat 42.3 g
- Saturated Fat 26.7 g
- Cholesterol 144 mg
- Total Carbs 12.7 g
- Sugar 5.6 g
- Fibre 4.5 g
- Sodium 148 mg
- Potassium 397 mg
- *Protein 4.2 g*

Cheesy Broccoli and Cauliflower

Prep Time: 10 minutes

Cooking Time: 10 minutes

Servings: 4

Ingredients:

- 8 oz. cauliflower, chopped
- 1 lb. broccoli, chopped
- 5 1/3 oz. shredded cheese
- 2 oz. butter
- 4 tablespoons sour cream
- salt and pepper

Method:

1. Melt butter in a large skillet and stir in all the vegetables.
2. Sauté over medium-high heat until golden brown.
3. Add all the remaining ingredients to the vegetables.
4. Mix well then serve.

Nutritional Information per Serving:

- Calories 244
- Total Fat 20.4 g
- Saturated Fat 67 g
- Cholesterol 130 mg
- Total Carbs 3.4 g
- Sugar 1 g
- Fibre 0.8 g
- Sodium 506 mg
- Potassium 217 mg
- *Protein 12.3 g*

Green Beans with Roasted Onions

Prep Time: 10 minutes

Cooking Time: 15 minutes

Servings: 6

Ingredients:

- 1 yellow onion, sliced into rings
- ½ teaspoon salt
- ½ teaspoon onion powder
- 2 tablespoons coconut flour
- 1 1/3 lbs. fresh green beans, trimmed and chopped

Method:

1. Mix salt with onion powder and coconut flour in a large bowl.
2. Add onion rings and mix well to coat.
3. Spread the rings in the baking sheet, lined with parchment paper.
4. Top them with some oil and bake for 10 minutes at 400F.
5. Meanwhile, parboil the green beans for 3 to 5 minutes in the boiling water.
6. Drain and serve the beans with baked onion rings.
7. Serve.

Nutritional Information per Serving:

- Calories 214
- Total Fat 19.4 g
- Saturated Fat 57 g
- Cholesterol 120 mg
- Total Carbs 3.7 g
- Sugar 0.8 g
- Fibre 0.3 g
- Sodium 343 mg

- Sugar 3.4 g
- Fibre 1.5 g
- Sodium 10 mg
- Potassium 178 mg
- *Protein 8.6 g*

Portobello Mushrooms

Prep Time: 10 minutes

Cooking Time: 10minutes

Servings: 4

Ingredients:

- 12 cherry tomatoes
- 2 oz. scallions
- 4 portabella mushrooms, stems removed
- 4¼ oz. butter or olive oil
- salt and pepper

Method:

1. Melt butter in a large skillet over medium heat.
2. Add mushrooms and sauté for 3 minutes.
3. Stir in cherry tomatoes and scallions.
4. Sauté for about 5 minutes.
5. Adjust seasoning with salt and pepper.
6. Sauté until vegetables are soft
7. Serve warm and enjoy.

Nutritional Information per Serving:

- Calories 154
- Total Fat 10.4 g
- Saturated Fat 57 g
- Cholesterol 110 mg
- Total Carbs 3.4 g
- Sugar 0.9 g
- Fibre 1.2 g
- Sodium 156 mg

- Potassium 120 mg
- *Protein 6.7 g*

Butter-fried Green Cabbage

Prep Time: 10 minutes

Cooking Time: 15 minutes

Servings: 4

Ingredients:

- 1½ lbs. shredded green cabbage
- 3 oz. butter
- salt to taste
- Freshly ground black pepper, to taste
- 1 dollop, whipped cream

Method:

1. Melt butter in a large skillet.
2. Stir in cabbage and sauté for about 15 minutes until golden brown.
3. Season with salt and pepper.
4. Serve warm with a dollop of cream.

Nutritional Information per Serving:

- Calories 199
- Total Fat 17.4 g
- Saturated Fat 11.3 g
- Cholesterol 47 mg
- Total Carbs 9.9 g
- Sugar 5.5 g
- Fibre 4.3 g
- Sodium 192 mg
- Potassium 296 mg
- Protein 2.4 g

Asian Garlic Tofu

Prep Time: 10 minutes

Cooking Time: 10minutes

Servings: 4

Ingredients:

- 1 package super firm tofu
- 1/4 cup Hoisin sauce
- 1 teaspoon ginger garlic paste
- 1/4 teaspoon red pepper flakes
- 1 teaspoon sesame oil
- Green onions, chopped (garnish)

Method:

1. Remove tofu from packaging. Place about 4 paper towels on a plate.
2. Place tofu on top of the plate and cover with more paper towels.
3. Place a heavy cast iron pan on top. Let sit 30 minutes.
4. Mix all the remaining ingredients in a bowl and set it aside.
5. Slice the tofu into small cubes and transfer them to the marinade.
6. Mix well and marinate for 30 minutes.
7. Heat oil in a skillet and add tofu to the sauté until golden brown from all the sides.
8. Garnish with green onions.
9. Serve warm.

Nutritional Information per Serving:

- Calories 467
- Total Fat 28.5 g
- Saturated Fat 2.7 g
- Cholesterol 0 mg

- Total Carbs 17.4 g
- Sugar 6.7 g
- Fibre 2.9 g
- Sodium 320 mg
- Potassium 632 mg
- *Protein 45.9 g*

Stuffed Mushrooms

Prep Time: 10 minutes

Cooking Time: 15minutes

Servings: 4

Ingredients:

- 4 Portobello mushrooms
- 1 cup crumbled blue cheese
- fresh thyme
- 2 tbsp extra virgin olive oil
- salt to taste

Method:

1. Preheat the oven to 350 degrees F.
2. Remove the stems from the mushrooms and chop them into small pieces.
3. Mix stem pieces with blue cheese, thyme and salt in a bowl.
4. Stuff each mushroom with the prepared cheese filling.
5. Drizzle some oil on top and place the mushrooms in a baking sheet.
6. Bake for 15 to 20 minutes.
7. Serve warm.

Nutritional Information per Serving:

- Calories 124
- Total Fat 22.4 g
- Saturated Fat 17 g
- Cholesterol 30 mg
- Total Carbs 5.4 g
- Sugar 1.2 g
- Fibre 2.8 g
- Sodium 206 mg

- Potassium 227 mg

CHAPTER 8: KETOGENIC SIDE DISHES

Eggplant Salad

Prep Time: 10 minutes

Cooking Time: 30 minutes

Servings: 3

Ingredients:

- 2 eggplant, peeled and sliced
- 2 green bell peppers, sliced, seeds removed
- ½ cup mayonnaise
- ½ cup fresh parsley
- 2 garlic cloves
- Salt and black pepper to taste

Method:

1. Preheat your oven to 480ºF (250ºC).
2. Add bell pepper and eggplants to a baking pan.
3. Bake for half an hour and flip the vegetables after 20 minutes.
4. Add baked vegetables and all the remaining ingredients to a bowl.
5. Mix well and serve.

Nutritional Information per Serving:

- Calories 196
- Total Fat 10.4 g
- Saturated Fat 1.5 g
- Cholesterol 8 mg
- Total Carbs 13.4 g
- Sugar 1 g
- Fibre 0.8 g
- Sodium 226 mg

- Potassium 217 mg
- *Protein 14.3 g*

Mixed Cabbage Coleslaw

Prep Time: 10 minutes

Cooking Time: 0 minute

Servings: 6

Ingredients:

- 12 oz. green and red cabbage, shredded and mixed
- 4 oz. kale, chopped
- 1 cup mayonnaise
- ½ teaspoon salt
- ¼ teaspoon ground black pepper

Method:

1. Add all the ingredients to a larger bowl.
2. Mix well using a spatula.
3. Serve and enjoy.

Nutritional Information per Serving:

- Calories 266
- Total Fat 26.4 g
- Saturated Fat 4 g
- Cholesterol 13 mg
- Total Carbs 5.4 g
- Sugar 2 g
- Fibre 1.6 g
- Sodium 455 mg
- Potassium 94 mg
- *Protein 0.6 g*

Red Coleslaw

Prep Time: 10 minutes

Cooking Time: 0 minute

Servings: 4

Ingredients:

- 1 2/3 lbs. red cabbage
- 1 ¼ cups mayonnaise
- Salt and black pepper to taste
- 2 teaspoons ground caraway seeds
- 1 tablespoon whole-grain mustard

Method:

1. Add all the ingredients to a larger bowl.
2. Mix well using a spatula and let it sit for 10 minutes.
3. Serve and enjoy.

Nutritional Information per Serving:

- Calories 406
- Total Fat 40.4 g
- Saturated Fat 6.1 g
- Cholesterol 20 mg
- Total Carbs 10 g
- Sugar 5.1 g
- Fibre 4.4 g
- Sodium 406 mg
- Potassium 284 mg
- Protein 2.2 g

Roasted Tomato Salad

Prep Time: 10 minutes

Cooking Time: 25 minutes

Servings: 4

Ingredients:

- 3 tablespoons olive oil
- 1 lb. cherry tomatoes
- sea salt and ground black pepper, to taste
- ½ cup finely chopped scallions
- 1 tablespoon red wine vinegar

Method:

1. Season tomatoes with oil and spices.
2. Heat oven to 450 degrees F.
3. Spread the tomatoes in a baking sheet and bake for 15 minutes.
4. Stir and turn the tomatoes then bake for 10 minutes.
5. Mix the roasted tomatoes with all the remaining ingredients in a bowl.
6. Serve.

Nutritional Information per Serving:

- Calories 115
- Total Fat 10.4 g
- Saturated Fat 1.5 g
- Cholesterol 0 mg
- Total Carbs 5.4 g
- Sugar 3.3 g
- Fiber 1.7 g
- Sodium 110 mg
- Potassium 306 mg

- Protein 1.2 g

Caprese Salad

Prep Time: 10 minutes

Cooking Time: 0 minute

Servings: 4

Ingredients:

- 8 oz. cherry tomatoes, cut in half
- 8 oz. mozzarella, mini cheese balls, cut in half
- 2 tablespoons green pesto
- Salt to taste
- Black pepper ground, to taste

Method:

1. Add all the ingredients to a larger bowl.
2. Mix well using a spatula.
3. Serve and enjoy.

Nutritional Information per Serving:

- Calories 213
- Total Fat 23.4 g
- Saturated Fat 6.1 g
- Cholesterol 102 mg
- Total Carbs 4.5 g
- Sugar 2.1 g
- Fibre 1.5 g
- Sodium 86 mg
- Potassium 297 mg
- *Protein 1.2 g*

Keto Kohlslaws

Prep Time: 10 minutes

Cooking Time: 0 minute

Servings: 4

Ingredients:

- 1 lb. kohlrabi, peeled and shredded
- 1 cup mayonnaise
- Salt to taste
- Ground black pepper, to taste
- fresh parsley, chopped

Method:

1. Add all the ingredients to a bowl.
2. Mix well until well combined.
3. Adjust seasoning with salt and pepper.
4. Serve and enjoy.

Nutritional Information per Serving:

- Calories 392
- Total Fat 40.4 g
- Saturated Fat 6 g
- Cholesterol 20 mg
- Total Carbs 7.2 g
- Sugar 3 g
- Fibre 4.2 g
- Sodium 423 mg
- Potassium 411 mg
- Protein 2 g

Goat Cheese Salad

Prep Time: 10 minutes

Cooking Time: 35minutes

Servings: 4

Ingredients:

- 10 oz. goat cheese, sliced
- 4 tablespoons pumpkin seeds
- 2 oz. butter
- 1 tablespoon balsamic vinegar
- 3 oz. baby spinach

Method:

1. Preheat your oven to 400°F (200°C).
2. Spread cheese slices in the baking dish and bake for 10 minutes.
3. Add pumpkin seeds to a skillet and roast until they change their colour.
4. Reduce the heat and add butter.
5. Let it simmer until butter is golden brown.
6. Add vinegar and bring the mixture to a boil.
7. Turn off the heat and stir in spinach.
8. Let it sit for 5 minutes and transfer to the platter.
9. Top the salad with baked cheese.

Nutritional Information per Serving:

- Calories 474
- Total Fat 40.8 g
- Saturated Fat 25.5 g
- Cholesterol 105 mg
- Total Carbs 3.9 g

- Sugar 1.8 g
- Fibre 0.8 g
- Sodium 345 mg
- Potassium 228 mg
- *Protein 24.5 g*

Kale Salad

Prep Time: 10 minutes

Cooking Time: 5minutes

Servings: 4

Ingredients:

- ¾ cup coconut cream
- 1 tablespoon olive oil
- 1 garlic clove, minced or finely chopped
- salt and pepper, to taste
- 2 oz. butter
- 8 oz. kale, rinsed and chopped

Method:

1. Mix cream with mayonnaise, oil, garlic, salt and pepper in a bowl.
2. Melt butter in the skillet and add kale to sauté until it turns colour.
3. Add kale to the mayo dressing and mix well.
4. Top with blue cheese and serve.

Nutritional Information per Serving:

- Calories 238
- Total Fat 23.2 g
- Saturated Fat 13 g
- Cholesterol 61 mg
- Total Carbs 6.8 g
- Sugar 0 g
- Fibre 0.9 g
- Sodium 115 mg
- Potassium 303 mg
- *Protein 2.3 g*

CHAPTER 9: KETOGENIC SNACKS

Halloumi Fries with Avocado Dip

Prep Time: 10 minutes

Cooking Time: 20 minutes

Servings: 2

Ingredients:

- 6 oz. halloumi cheese, cut it lengthwise sticks
- oil for frying
- Avocado Dip
- 1 avocado, peeled and pit removed
- ½ cup sour cream or crème fraiche
- salt and ground black pepper

Method:

1. Place avocado flesh into a bowl and mash it coarsely using a fork.
2. Add all the remaining ingredients of the dip to the bowl. Mix well and set it aside.
3. Use a paper towel to pat dry the halloumi sticks.
4. Heat oil in a deep pan to 350 F.
5. Add halloumi sticks to the oil and cook until golden brown.
6. Serve warm with avocado dip.

Nutritional Information per Serving:

- Calories 349
- Total Fat 31.9 g
- Saturated Fat 15 g
- Cholesterol 46 mg
- Total Carbs 6.6 g
- Sugar 1.4 g

- Fibre 3.4 g
- Sodium 237 mg
- Potassium 352 mg
- *Protein 11 g*

Ranch Dip

Prep Time: 10 minutes

Cooking Time: 0 minute

Servings: 8

Ingredients:

- 1 cup mayonnaise
- 8 tablespoons crème fraiche or sour cream
- 2 tablespoons ranch seasoning
- Salt to taste
- Black pepper to taste

Method:

1. Add all the ingredients to a bowl.
2. Mix well until well combined.
3. Cover the bowl and refrigerate for 15 minutes.
4. Serve and enjoy.

Nutritional Information per Serving:

- Calories 148
- Total Fat 12.3 g
- Saturated Fat 3 g
- Cholesterol 13 mg
- Total Carbs 7.5 g
- Sugar 1.9 g
- Fibre 0 g
- Sodium 403 mg
- Potassium 20 mg
- Protein 0.6 g

Spicy Roasted Nuts

Prep Time: 10 minutes

Cooking Time: 5 minutes

Servings: 6

Ingredients:

- 8 oz. pecans or almonds or walnuts
- 1 teaspoon salt
- 1 tablespoon olive oil or coconut oil
- 1 teaspoon ground cumin
- 1 teaspoon paprika powder or chilli powder

Method:

1. Add all the ingredients to a skillet.
2. Roast the nuts until golden brown.
3. Serve and enjoy.

Nutritional Information per Serving:

- Calories 287
- Total Fat 29.5 g
- Saturated Fat 3 g
- Cholesterol 0 mg
- Total Carbs 5.9 g
- Sugar 1.4g
- Fibre 4.3 g
- Sodium 388 mg
- Potassium 163 mg
- Protein 4.2 g

Salad Sandwiches

Prep Time: 10 minutes

Cooking Time: 0 minute

Servings: 1

Ingredients:

- 2 oz. Romaine lettuce or baby gem lettuce rinsed
- ½ oz. butter
- 1 oz. Adam cheese, sliced
- ½ avocado, sliced
- 1 cherry tomatoes, sliced

Method:

1. Add butter on top of each lettuce leaves.
2. Add alternate layers of cheese, avocado and tomato slices on top of lettuce leaves.
3. Serve and enjoy.

Nutritional Information per Serving:

- Calories 104
- Total Fat 14.7 g
- Saturated Fat 3.7 g
- Cholesterol 32 mg
- Total Carbs 5.6 g
- Sugar 2.4 g
- Fibre 1.1 g
- Sodium 241 mg
- Potassium 148 mg
- Protein 4.3 g

Baked Onion Rings

Prep Time: 10 minutes

Cooking Time: 25 minutes

Servings: 4

Ingredients:

- 1 egg
- 1 jumbo onion, peeled and sliced into rings
- 1 cup almond flour
- ½ tablespoon chilli powder or paprika powder
- 1 pinch salt
- 1 tablespoon olive oil

Method:

1. Preheat the oven to 400°F (200°C).
2. Add all the dry ingredients to a bowl. Mix well
3. Whisk eggs in another bowl.
4. First, dip each ring into the egg batter then coat it with dry mixture.
5. Arrange all the onion rings on a baking sheet lined with parchment paper.
6. Drizzle oil on top then bake them for 15 to 20 minutes.
7. Serve warm.

Nutritional Information per Serving:

- Calories 184
- Total Fat 19.1 g
- Saturated Fat 7.7 g
- Cholesterol 35 mg
- Total Carbs 10.5 g
- Sugar 1.8 g
- Fibre 5.3 g

- Sodium 141 mg
- Potassium 178 mg
- *Protein 5.6 g*

Roasted Green Beans

Prep Time: 10 minutes

Cooking Time: 20 minutes

Servings: 4

Ingredients:

- 1 egg
- 2 tablespoons olive oil
- Salt and Black pepper to taste
- 1 lb. fresh green beans
- 5 1/3 tablespoons grated parmesan cheese

Method:

1. Preheat the oven to 400°F (200°C).
2. Whisk eggs with oil and spices in a bowl.
3. Add beans and mix well.
4. Stir in parmesan cheese and pour this mixture into the baking pan, lined with parchment paper.
5. Bake for about 15 to 20 minutes in the top rack of the oven.
6. Serve warm

Nutritional Information per Serving:

- Calories 216
- Total Fat 21.7 g
- Saturated Fat 6.1 g
- Cholesterol 16 mg
- Total Carbs 7.1 g
- Sugar 2.4 g
- Fibre 0.6 g
- Sodium 111 mg

- Potassium 128 mg
- *Protein 8.9 g*

CHAPTER 10: KETOGENIC SOUPS

Cheesy Broccoli Soup

Prep Time: 10 minutes

Cooking Time: 4 hours

Servings: 3

Ingredients:

- 1 cup broccoli
- 1 cup vegetable broth
- 1 cup cheddar cheese
- ½ cup coconut cream
- Salt, to taste

Method:

1. Add all the ingredients to a crock pot.
2. Cook for 4 hours on low settings.
3. Serve warm.

Nutritional Information per Serving:

- Calories 215
- Total Fat 21.4 g
- Saturated Fat 67 g
- Cholesterol 123 mg
- Total Carbs 9.4 g
- Sugar 0.3 g
- Fibre 2.8 g
- Sodium 156 mg
- Potassium 317 mg
- *Protein 3.5 g*

Roasted Garlic Soup

Prep Time: 10 minutes

Cooking Time: 60 minutes

Servings: 10

Ingredients:

- 1 tablespoon olive oil
- 2 bulbs of garlic, peeled
- 3 shallots, chopped
- 1 large head of cauliflower, chopped (approximately 5 cups)
- 6 cups gluten-free vegetable broth
- Salt and ground pepper, to taste

Method:

1. Preheat the oven to 400F.
2. Slice ¼-inch top of the garlic bulb and place in an aluminium foil.
3. Grease with some olive oil and roast for 35 minutes in the oven
4. Squeeze the flesh out of roasted garlic.
5. Heat oil in a saucepan and add shallots to sauté for 6 minutes.
6. Add garlic and all the remaining ingredients.
7. Cover the pan and reduce the heat to low
8. Let it cook for 15 to 20 minutes.
9. Use a handheld blender to puree the mixture.
10. Season the soup with salt and pepper.
11. Serve warm.

Nutritional Information per Serving:

- Calories 142

- Total Fat 8.4 g
- Saturated Fat 67 g
- Cholesterol 130 mg
- Total Carbs 3.4 g
- Sugar 1 g
- Fibre 0.8 g
- Sodium 346 mg
- Potassium 382 mg
- *Protein 4.1 g*

Greens Soup

Prep Time: 10 minutes

Cooking Time: 0 minute

Servings: 6

Ingredients:

- 2 cups spinach leaves
- 1 avocado, peeled and diced
- 1/2 cup English cucumber, peeled and diced
- 1/4 cup gluten-free vegetable broth
- Salt freshly ground pepper, to taste

Method:

1. Blend all the ingredients in the blender.
2. Garnish with fresh herbs.
3. Serve and enjoy.

Nutritional Information per Serving:

- Calories 191
- Total Fat 8.4 g
- Saturated Fat 0.7 g
- Cholesterol 0 mg
- Total Carbs 7.1 g
- Sugar 0.1 g
- Fibre 1.4 g
- Sodium 226 mg
- Potassium 323 mg
- Protein 6.3 g

Kale and Spinach Soup

Prep Time: 5 minutes

Cooking Time: 10 minutes

Servings: 4

Ingredients:

- 3 oz. coconut oil
- 8 oz. kale, chopped
- 2 avocados, diced
- 4 1/3 cups coconut milk or coconut cream
- Salt and ground black pepper, to taste

Method:

1. Heat oil in a skillet and add kale to sauté for 2 to 3 minutes.
2. Add kale to a blender along with water, spices, coconut milk and avocado.
3. Blend well until smooth then transfer it to a bowl.
4. Serve.

Nutritional Information per Serving:

- Calories 124
- Total Fat 13.4 g
- Saturated Fat 7 g
- Cholesterol 20 mg
- Total Carbs 11.4 g
- Sugar 2.1 g
- Fibre 4.8 g
- Sodium 136 mg
- Potassium 427 mg
- Protein 4.2 g

Cauliflower Soup

Prep Time: 10 minutes

Cooking Time: 10 minutes

Servings: 6

Ingredients:

- 4 cups vegetable stock
- 1 lb. cauliflower, trimmed and chopped
- 7 oz. cream cheese
- 4 oz. butter
- salt and pepper to taste

Method:

1. Heat butter in a skillet and add cauliflower to sauté for 2 minutes.
2. Add stock and bring the mixture to a boil. Cook until the cauliflower is al dente
3. Stir in cream cheese, salt and pepper.
4. Puree the mixture using a hand-held blender.
5. Serve warm.

Nutritional Information per Serving:

- Calories 143
- Total Fat 16.7 g
- Saturated Fat 9.7 g
- Cholesterol 32 mg
- Total Carbs 8.6 g
- Sugar 2.4 g
- Fibre 5.7 g
- Sodium 141 mg
- Potassium 478 mg
- *Protein 3.4 g*

Mushroom Soup

Prep Time: 10 minutes

Cooking Time: 30 minutes

Servings: 4

Ingredients:

- 4 oz. butter
- 1 lb. mushrooms
- 7 oz. cream cheese
- 3 cups water
- 1 cup coconut cream
- Salt and black pepper to taste

Method:

1. Heat butter in a saucepan and add mushrooms.
2. Sauté until golden brown in colour. Adjust seasoning with salt and pepper
3. Add cream cheese and water to the pan and bring the mixture to a boil.
4. Reduce the heat and let it simmer for 15 minutes.
5. Beat the cream in an electric mixer until creamy.
6. Add cream to the soup and gently fold it in.
7. Puree the mixture using a hand-held blender.
8. Serve warm and enjoy.

Nutritional Information per Serving:

- Calories 134
- Total Fat 11.4 g
- Saturated Fat 1.2 g
- Cholesterol 0 mg
- Total Carbs 10.1 g

- Sugar 2.7 g
- Fibre 5.2 g
- Sodium 10 mg
- Potassium 557 mg
- *Protein 2.3 g*

Avocado-Cucumber Gazpacho

Servings: 6

Prep Time: 10 minutes

Cooking Time: 0 minute

Ingredients:

- 2 medium cucumbers peeled, seeded, and chopped
- 1 1/2 avocados chopped
- 1/3 cup loosely packed cilantro or basil leaves
- Salt and pepper, to taste
- 1 to 1 1/2 cups water

Method:

1. Add all the ingredients to a blender.
2. Blend well and adjust seasoning with salt and pepper.
3. Serve and enjoy.

Nutritional Information per Serving:

- Calories 131
- Total Fat 10.4 g
- Saturated Fat 9.5 g
- Cholesterol 10 mg
- Total Carbs 9.1 g
- Sugar 0.5 g
- Fibre 3.4 g
- Sodium 106 mg
- Potassium 417 mg
- *Protein 2.3 g*

CHAPTER 11: KETOGENIC DESSERT RECIPES

Chocolate Peanut Butter Cups

Prep Time: 10 minutes

Cooking Time: 30 minutes

Servings: 5

Ingredients:

- 2 ounces unsweetened chocolate
- ¼ cup heavy cream
- 4 packets erythritol
- 1 cup butter
- ¼ cup peanut butter, separated

Method:

1. Preheat the oven to 360 degrees F.
2. Melt the butter and peanut butter in a bowl.
3. Stir in erythritol, unsweetened chocolate and heavy cream.
4. Mix thoroughly and put the mixture in a baking mould.
5. Put the baking mould in the oven.
6. Bake for 30 minutes and dish out.

Nutritional Information per Serving:

- *Calories 479*
- *Total Fat 51.5 g*
- *Saturated Fat 29.7 g*
- *Cholesterol 106 mg*
- *Total Carbs 7.7 g*
- *Sugar 1.4 g*
- *Fibre 2.7 g*
- *Sodium 69 mg*

- *Potassium 193 mg*
- *Protein 5.2 g*

Chocolate Brownies

Prep Time: 10 minutes

Cooking Time: 30 minutes

Servings: 4

Ingredients:

- ½ cup sugar-free chocolate chips
- ½ cup butter
- 1 teaspoon vanilla extract
- 3 eggs
- ¼ cup erythritol

Method:

1. Preheat your oven to 395 degrees F and grease a baking dish.
2. Beat eggs with erythritol and vanilla extract
3. Blend well until fluffy.
4. Melt chocolate with butter in the microwave and mix well.
5. Add chocolate melt to the egg batter.
6. Stir gently and pour the batter into the baking dish
7. Bake for about 30 minutes and allow it to cool.
8. Cut it into squares and serve with whipped cream.

Nutritional Information per Serving:

- *Calories 266*
- *Total Fat 26.9 g*
- *Saturated Fat 15.8 g*
- *Cholesterol 184 mg*
- *Total Carbs 2.5 g*
- *Sugar 0.4 g*
- *Fibre 0 g*

- Sodium 218 mg
- Potassium 53 mg
- Protein 4.5 g

Cream Crepes

Prep Time: 10 minutes

Cooking Time: 16 minutes

Servings: 4

Ingredients:

- 2 tablespoons coconut flour
- 2 organic eggs
- 2 tablespoons coconut oil, melted and divided
- 1/3 cup coconut cream
- 1 teaspoon Splenda

Method:

1. Blend eggs with Splenda and coconut oil until creamy.
2. Gradually add coconut flour to the egg mixture.
3. Stir in cream and beat well until mixed.
4. Add the coconut flour slowly while continuously beating.
5. Pour ¼ of this batter in a skillet and cook on low heat for 2 minutes per side.
6. Cook more pancakes using three batches of batter.
7. Serve with whipped cream.

Nutritional Information per Serving:

- Calories 145
- Total Fat 13.1 g
- Saturated Fat 9.1 g
- Cholesterol 96 mg
- Total Carbs 4 g
- Sugar 1.2 g
- Fibre 1.5 g
- Sodium 35 mg

- Potassium 37 mg
- *Protein 3.5 g*

Lemon Mousse

Prep Time: 10 minutes

Cooking Time: 10 minutes

Servings: 4

Ingredients:

- 1 cup coconut cream
- 8-ounces cream cheese softened
- ¼ cup fresh lemon juice
- 3 pinches salt
- 1 teaspoon lemon liquid stevia

Method:

1. Preheat your oven to 350 degrees F and butter a ramekin.
2. Beat cream with cream cheese, fresh lemon juice, salt and lemon liquid stevia in a mixer.
3. Pour the batter into the ramekin.
4. Bake for about 10 minutes then transfer the mousse to the serving glass.
5. Refrigerate for 2 hours and serve.

Nutritional Information per Serving:

- Calories 305
- Total Fat 31 g
- Saturated Fat 19.5 g
- Cholesterol 103 mg
- Total Carbs 2.7 g
- Sugar 0.5 g
- Fibre 0.1 g
- Sodium 299 mg
- Potassium 109 mg

- *Protein 5 g*

Chocolate Cheese Cake

Prep Time: 10 minutes

Cooking Time: 12 minutes

Servings: 3

Ingredients:

- 1 cup cream cheese, softened
- 1 egg
- 1 tablespoon cocoa powder
- ½ teaspoon pure vanilla extract
- ¼ cup Swerve

Method:

1. Preheat your oven to 350 degrees F.
2. Beat cream cheese with eggs in a blender until smooth.
3. Stir in swerve, cocoa powder and vanilla extract.
4. Beat well until mixed and pour the batter into two 8-ounce mason jars.
5. Bake for 12 minutes. Then allow it to cool.
6. Refrigerate for 5 hours.
7. Serve.

Nutritional Information per Serving:

- Calories 244
- Total Fat 24.8 g
- Saturated Fat 15.6 g
- Cholesterol 32 mg
- Total Carbs 2.1 g
- Sugar 0.4 g
- Fibre 0.1 g
- Sodium 204 mg

- Potassium 81 mg
- *Protein 4 g*

Peanut Butter Pudding

Prep Time: 10 minutes

Cooking Time: 10 minutes

Servings: 4

Ingredients:

- 2 cups cashew milk, unsweetened
- 2 teaspoons gelatin
- ½ cup cold water
- 2 tablespoons swerve
- ¼ cup natural peanut butter

Method:

1. Combine cashew milk with peanut butter and swerve in a bowl.
2. Add this mixture to a saucepan and cook for 5 minutes on medium heat.
3. Mix water with gelatin in a small bowl.
4. Add gelatin to the saucepan and stir cook for 5 minutes.
5. Let it stand for 1 hour.
6. Pour the pudding into the serving bowls.
7. Refrigerate for 4 hours.
8. Serve.

Nutritional Information per Serving:

- Calories 124
- Total Fat 9 g
- Saturated Fat 1.5 g
- Cholesterol 0 mg
- Total Carbs 4.5 g
- Sugar 1 g
- Fibre 1 g

- Sodium 91 mg
- Potassium 13 mg
- *Protein 8 g*

CONCLUSION:

Vegetarians, who were ever been troubled with the idea of pure ketogenic diet, can now get the best of it using given compilation of all the vegetarian ketogenic recipes. Encompassing all the varieties of food, this book is a door to the keto world, for all the beginners out there. With some simple ingredients and strict routine give a big boost to ketosis in your body and experience its miraculous effects. However, expert's opinion, proper guidance, medical history and care should be taken into consideration before setting off on this journey. Besides a good diet plan and a complete meal chart, intake of fluids and exercises are equally important to harness the maximum effect of this diet. Incorporate the given recipes into different sets or combinations of the meal for each day so that you could experience variety along with unique and inspiring flavours. Whereas this book is here to guarantee that with minimum effort, lesser kitchen time and a bit of creativity, everyone can enjoy making their own scrumptious and healthy ketogenic meal right at home.

Made in the USA
San Bernardino, CA
16 August 2018